Use these stickers on your map of Never Land!

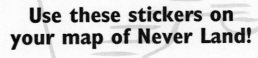

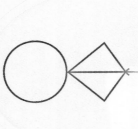

Use a glue stick or tape to place a picture of yourself here!

Never Land

Yo Ho, Let's Go!

Written by Bill Scollon
Illustrated by Alan Batson

Copyright © 2012 Disney Enterprises, Inc. All rights reserved. Published by Dalmatian Press, LLC, in conjunction with Disney Enterprises, Inc. Printed in the U.S.A.

20059 Jake and the Never Land Pirates Sticker Book to Color with Treasure Map
13 14 15 NGS 39101 10 9 8 7 6 5 4

Look what washed ashore!

"It's an underwater diving helmet!" says Izzy.

Connect the dots to complete the map of Never Land.

"I spy treasure!" says Captain Hook. **"I want to spoil their fun, so I must have that hat-buckety thing."**

Cubby is going to look at the fish.

Which fish is different?

Your Answer: [ ]

Answer: C

8

"Aha! I've got it! The treasure is mine!"

"Aw, coconuts!" says Cubby.

"The scallywags are headed for Seahorse Shallows!"
squawks Skully.

Write the location of the pictures on the grid as shown.

4

3

2

1

A   B   C   D

🪖 is at **B**,**4**   🚣 is at __,__   🐠 is at __,__

👧 is at __,__   🧔 is at __,__   👦 is at __,__

Answer: 1. (B, 4), 2. (D, 2), 3. (C, 1), 4. (B, 1), 5. (C, 3), 6. (A, 2)

"Look alive, crew! Yo ho, let's go!"

Captain Hook is underwater looking at the seahorses.

**Bucky can't get close to the shore.
The water is too shallow.**

Dalmatian Press

How many seahorses are swimming with Captain Hook?

Your Answer:

Draw lines to match the characters with their names.

 **A**

 **B**

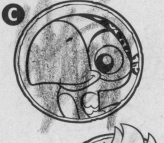 **C**

 **D**

 **E**

 **F**

❶ HOOK

❷ JAKE

❸ SMEE

❹ IZZY

❺ SKULLY

❻ CUBBY

Answer: A-1, B-4, C-5, D-2, E-6, F-3

"Follow me, mateys!" yells Izzy. They swing on ropes
off the ship to the beach. Smee is alarmed.

"We solved a Pirate Problem by getting to the beach and got 4 Gold Doubloons! Let's grab 'em and go!"

"I'm keeping the hat-bucket thingy!" says Hook.

Why does Captain Hook
want to keep the hat-bucket thingy?
Use the code to find out.

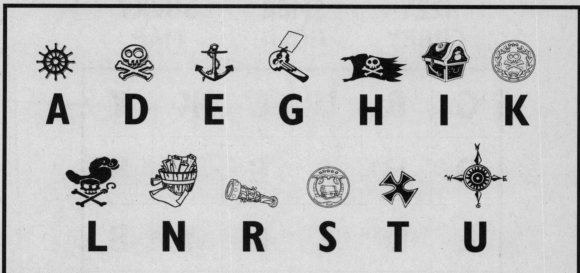

A D E G H I K

L N R S T U

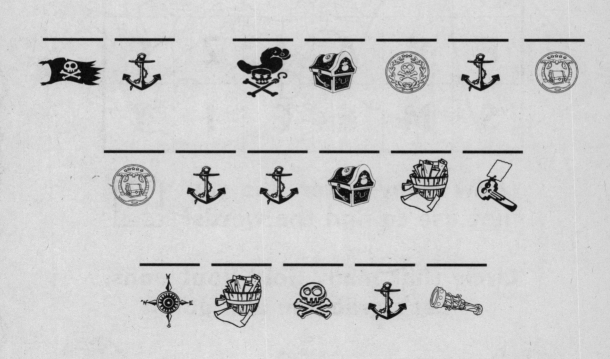

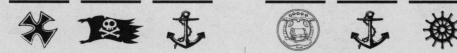

Look up, down, across, and diagonally for these Never Land words.

JAKE	HOOK	SKULLY
IZZY	SMEE	BUCKY
CUBBY	GOLD	MAP

G	B	U	C	K	Y
O	H	A	B	L	B
L	O	C	L	Y	B
D	O	U	P	Z	U
E	K	A	J	Z	C
S	M	E	E	I	Y

How many letters did you <u>not</u> use to find the words?

Circle that many Gold Doubloons. Let's grab 'em and go!

Use the grid
to draw Skully.

Skully grabs the helmet.
"Cheese and crackers! I've got it!"

"Great work, Skully! We got 2 Gold Doubloons!
Let's grab 'em and go!"

Can you follow the clues to solve the crossword puzzle?

ACROSS:

2. Jake and his crew find a diving _____.

4. Hook wants to _____ their fun.

6. _____ steals the helmet!

DOWN:

1. Another word for beach is _____ .

3. Cubby saw _____ under the water.

5. _____ swings on a rope to the shore.

"Barnacles!"

How many words can you think of that rhyme with:

HOOK   **SMEE**

_____   _____

_____   _____

_____   _____

_____   _____

_____   _____

_____   _____

Possible answers: HOOK: book, brook, cook, crook, look, nook, rook, shook, took. SMEE: bee, flee/flea, glee, he, key, me, knee, pea, sea/see, tea, tree, we.

"This is all your fault, Smee!" says Hook.

"Back to Pirate Island, me hearties!"

Help Jake put the Gold Doubloons in the Team Treasure Chest.

START

How many do you count?

Answer: 10

Yo ho, way to go!

Have fun with these stickers—anywhere you like!